Conversations With Richard

Conversations With Richard

It's Not Over When You Die

Ann Weber

An Off the Common Book, Amherst, Massachusetts

© 2019 Ann I. Weber

cover photo:
Statue of Merlin the Wizard, town of Carmarthen, Wales, UK
Contributor: Charles Stirling / Alamy Stock Photo

An Off the Common Book, Amherst, Massachusetts

Printed in the United States of America

ISBN: 978-1-7332651-0-2

For
Dorothy and Sister Elizabeth

Foreword by Richard

I was born in Wales and carried with me throughout my life many of the fine qualities often found in those with this heritage, e.g., musicality, a theatrical speaking voice, and a poetical turn of mind. Unfortunately, I also nurtured a raging ego and a love for strong drink. As a result, my life was a series of rolling disasters in a flamboyant and public style peculiarly my own. Now that I am dead, I can't say that I have actually repented these excesses, but, suffice it to say, that I have felt the need to redeem a life which could have been an uncommonly gifted one which I instead allowed to career grievously out of control. In making public this communication with Ann, I hope to allow you who are still in mortal form to see beyond your sojourn in time-bound consciousness.

Ann presented a golden opportunity for me, for, not only was she able to hear my voice, but, after her initial incredulity, she called me on every feint and dodge that I tried to put by her, and thus forced me to grapple with issues I had previously shunted aside. Somehow she was not impressed by my consequence, so what follows is a communication of equals, both struggling to come to terms with the finite human condition against which we have each in our own ways railed in vain. Come with us on this odd little journey undertaken by two spirits, one "dead" and one still "alive," toward a recognition and reconciliation of the human and divine within each of us, and perhaps make it your journey too. And in the process, have some fun. We certainly did.

Preface

I can't exactly recall when I first heard Richard's voice as set down here, but at first I assumed it to be some sort of fantasy. However, as his voice and presence became more insistent, there was a shock of recognition, for indeed this resonant voice was very well known and one I had heard as a child on a record my parents liked to play. Still, I thought, this is silly. But he would not go away. He intruded in moments when I settled down to do some quiet work of my own, when I was driving or making supper. He sang poetry to me, sometimes silly, sometimes serious. He declaimed and teased until I suspended disbelief and began to write down what I heard.

I have always had some form of clairaudient abilities, and for many years I have been inclined to ask questions of Spirit and receive answers which I heard in my mind and transcribed as they occurred. The words come so quickly that I cannot not tell what is being said until I read what I wrote later. And so I started writing what I heard from Richard. Then reading. And I was blown away.

Thinking that either I was losing my mind or something very extraordinary was happening, I checked in first with a psychic and then, to cover all bases, a well-respected

Catholic Sister. The psychic saw an image of a person that neither she nor anyone else would connect to Richard—but I did because I had just seen an obscure clip of Richard and this person on the internet. The Sister said, oh yes, this does happen, quite the blessing, not that unusual, she had given workshops on this, and I should follow it out.

Not that unusual. OK. Well, maybe not for her. Clearly I was out of my league here. But I did follow because there seemed to be no choice. In the process I found my way to Richard's little-known film *Circle of Two* about an older man who falls in love with a young girl, but, because of the depth of his love, he can take no action that would harm her. The film was not well-received, but it touched a nerve and formed the basis of our first interactions. In the process he offered wisdom and insight into the human condition not just as related to our two little lives but to the transformation that comes to us all in this life and beyond. As he did so, it became clear that the gift of these conversations could not be meant for me alone. So I began to put this little book together and hope it gives you something you are looking for.

By way of disclaimer, though I did know of Richard before commencing these writings, as he was a well-known actor prior to his death, I had no particular interest in or attraction to him and had never seen any of his movies or theater performances. (Sorry, Richard.)

The conversation with Richard
begins as follows…

1. March 24, 2015

Am I having sex therapy with a dead person?

Oh yes and very enjoyable it has been, wish we could have connected in the flesh so to speak.

Thank you for showing up.

My pleasure.

You found me.

Yes.

Do you do this for a living?

Always. (Laughing.)

The film *Circle of Two*?

Yes, more than anyone thought, the X relationship, he goes down while she goes up, but arrested by love. Not beautifully executed but something there. I'm glad it touched you.

Healed me. You said what I needed to hear.

And I am saying again to you. I love you; you are loved in all your craggy corners and blind transitions. I did what I wanted to do, felt what I needed to feel, and it cleansed me with all that suffering.

Will you come back?

No, not so you will see me, but I will see you anon. Goodbye.

2. March 24, 2015 - April 21, 2015. During this period I got no conversations but the following poems instead.

Circle of Two

What do you know now
That was held back before?
Since you're dead,
Would you be kind enough to share?
Or have you already
When you took my hand,
Held my body in all its perversions
And allowed me to hold you in my heart?
Two who did not like to be touched,
Content in utero together,
I want to linger in that amniotic state,
But that's not why you came
Or why I received you.
The sea change has occurred.
Two are one, then two again,
But never the same, thank God.

Crapshoot

Who's crazier, you or me?
I vote for me since I'm talking to you,
But you're coming up fast on the outside—
Or is it the inside,
Since, after all, you're dead
Which means you have a license to steal
Since nobody here knows what dead means.
But after all, I am the one writing this
So I think I win.

Oh, do you now?
Well, I'll see your crazy
And raise you by drink, death, and disloyalty.
Why else do you think I can see your little sins
As part of the whole,
The whole He gave us?
We do the best we can,
Angels can do no more.

In Excelsis

And so I asked him if he were real,
That long-dead spirit now in my head
And, more, in my essence.
And he laughed as at a private joke
That only we could share.
Could it be that healing comes
In a series of coincidences
Engineered by the dead
And prompted by my need?
In any case, someone came,
Entered, cauterized, nourished,
Then ascended in a shower of angels.

Conversations

We are blurring the lines
Between life and death,
You and I,
As we talk to each other.
You would laugh in disbelief or worse
To be considered a guide
So perhaps we can just be friends
And talk to each other
Though, as T. S. Eliot (I think) said
I am not worthy, I am not worthy.
So I will just have to get over it
Because it's too much fun to miss.
Who else gets to talk with a dead soul
Steeped in compassion, eloquence, and sin,
And have him talk back?

The Serpent's Question

Why should I be so special
That you should come to me
When all the world and its bright lights
Had prior claim?

You invited me in and held nothing back
Of all that appalls you.
So I too could claim a place to rest
In your undemanding arms
And give something back
That too many souls have squandered on me.
And when you received me, let me see you,
I saw that it was not wasted,
That the gifts I received
Go on through you
And back to me.

3. April 21, 2015

Thank you. I find it hard to believe it's you, that you would, could come and that you saw a kindred spirit in me. Will you tell me how this happened?

Yes, as far as I can. In life I suffered, pushed on, suffered, pushed on, but never changed my pattern. I needed to blast through life in my own way. I needed the highs, the adrenaline, the power, the excitement to keep me alive, to keep me from looking around, to keep me from reflecting. I never held a problem long in my mind and just moved on to the next matter, person, conquest, challenge, excitement, game, lover, role, person, experience. Living in the present, yes, but while I did so the wounds I ignored festered beneath the frail bandage of frenetic activity.

But you were given this energy, this sexual drive and this genius-level talent. Surely you knew you had something special in your own person?

No. I knew I had power, but I did not understand where it came from, was always afraid it would desert me. So I had to continually challenge it to be sure it was still there and I was still alive. Yet I knew that I had committed crimes against God, humanity, and those I loved the most, and so I accepted the Faustian bargain that I had made and took the consequences as the price to be paid for choosing my own pleasure without regard to others. I accepted and kept going. I don't know what would have happened if I had stopped and looked at my life. Much of it was just following out the next thing with no driver behind the wheel, just the next thing that fed my passion, my power and my continual highs.

Yes, but you gave to your loved ones of your heart, you never abandoned them or judged them. This too was who you were and in so doing you offered unconditional love to others even as you refused it for yourself.

I could not see this, but I made communion with my family, and I knew I was there for them, though never enough. I killed my brother, I ruined his life, and nothing I could do could atone so I went for oblivion in perpetual movement, drink, sex and adrenaline.

You have a very different temperament, but you too use a persistent pattern to block true feeling and experience, to keep yourself from experiencing the monster you have believed yourself to be, the Ill-Made Knight as that seer Tim White taught us. I see you dashing yourself against the bars of your self-made cage with the unspoken conviction that freedom is worse than self-immolation, that you are not worthy.

I am here to tell you that you are wrong, that freedom is your birthright and was mine too, but you still have time to claim yours in this lifetime, and as you do so, I too shall be freed. I move now within you and beside you, friend, lover, and scout on the path that I have trod before you. In our odd ways we are fellow travelers. Your addictions are less obvious but perhaps no less powerful than mine, but you have lived longer and you have asked for contact with the Divine beyond what your own efforts have brought you in the excitement of pitting yourself against the universe. You have begun to break the bonds of self-loathing and revulsion. I want to help you with this because my perspective allows me to see where we misunderstood.

I know that you want off this horse, this pattern that runs your life and has you in its grip. I never could see the possibility of a different course, as I thought I had chosen my path and must cleave to it. Now I have a wider view and, though I do not regret my life, I want a deeper connection with what we used to call God, and, in helping you, I travel at your shoulder and will claim the journey for my own if you will permit me to accompany you. We are kindred spirits. I offer you absolution, the knowledge that human experience is transitory but real in all its varied colours, from the brilliant to the repugnant, from the Divine to the profane and obscene. All is part of the experience. You need not cut yourself off from the darker side in order to be a child of God. You need not make the bargain and condemn yourself to eternal hell as I did, for such does not exist. You are whole as you are, in the flesh and in spirit. There is no separation from the love of Christ. I act now for you, for the other only, but, as altruism serves the giver, also for myself.

This is really weird.

It is, isn't it? That's what makes it fun.

4. April 23, 2015

Will you talk to me about why you did not want to be touched?

No, not now.

Should I not have shared you? You have withdrawn.

No, you needed to be validated by your friends who make their parallel journeys back to Spirit, but this is not group sex, so to speak. Let us keep the rest to ourselves just at present. Voyeurs will not help our cause.

OK, so sorry, I didn't see what it would do, the ego that it would spark in me, that it might feel like a déjà vu betrayal to you and how it would affect us. It has been a little hard to take all of this in stride, so I guess I will just have to lengthen my stride. Are we OK, can we still be together?

Yes, I will stay with you, just you for now.

A sacred place.

Yes.

5. April 24, 2015

Would you like to talk with me now?

Yes. Delighted you turned off that interview, I was a pompous ass.

Really? What makes you say so?

Pontificating. Although when you do those interviews, you have to say something, and they ask such ridiculous questions. Did I enjoy being famous! Well of course I did, and I hated it too. What an idiot!

You seem to have given up pontificating in favor of charitable work.

Oh you mean you, do you? No, no, quite the pleasure actually. And we're rowing along together for our mutual benefit. You should be up there sorting out your new meditation room instead of chatting to me.

I thought you appreciated friends who didn't nag.

Yes, but that was then and this is now, though I doubt I'll be much good as a nag. Instead, let me ask you what you're hoping to get from our association.

Good company, fun, insight from your—I won't say unique but certainly generally unavailable—perspective. And to have a friend to talk to, to be with through this, for lack of a better word, cleansing.

If you're looking for a spiritual guide, you've come to the wrong place. But I think I know what you mean. Suffering is cleansing, as I found to my dismay. Failure, murder, destruction by drink can be cleansing when reviewed from the perspective in which I now sit.

Do you regret it? You were given a hot rod, and you didn't leave it in the garage. What were your other choices?

Well, in regard to choice, I'm told we have one but I just plunged on, pulled back from the precipice over and over again until my body finally said "enough." And very glad of it I was, as I don't think I would have been good at being an old man.

King Lear?

Well yes, there was that carrot, there's regret.

Why does everyone say that's the greatest Shakespeare play? He seems like the silliest man not being able to tell his good daughter from the other two, if memory serves, which it may not as it's been decades since I read it.

Why don't you go back and do so again? Get one of those little commentary things to help you through, and then we can discuss.

OK, but I am not up to your weight.

No, but you bring something else to the table, fresh eyes. I think you will find upon further review that Lear is grappling with many of your own issues, inevitable decay, disillusionment, pervasive evil, which, despite all efforts to slay it, comes back like a particularly pestilent weed. Read it again and let me know what you think.

OK. It looks like I am going to be moving off my usual pabulum in the reading department if I hang around you.

Pabulum is nice. Both of us used reading to keep the world at bay, particularly that part of the world which can make us feel, hurt, cry, and rage against the dying of the light.

Did you rage?

Of course I did. I never did anything else. Always back into the fray, charge and charge again until finally I fell, hopefully in battle. I didn't exactly, but near enough, thank God.

I don't want to be old, lose my sight, not ride, read, move independently, play with my dogs.

No, a frightful prospect.

Don't you have any celestial wisdom, like God loves you, all will be well?

God loves you, all will be well.

Right.

We get what we need. Right now you have me.

An honor and a privilege.

And likewise. I can view our common issues from my celestial position on high and let you do all the work, an excellent program.

OK, I will go to work on the room.

Right.

I'm glad you didn't leave.

Me too.

6. April 25, 2015

Hi. Have been wanting to check in with you, see if you're there, feeling a little weird, not knowing what this is.

Well, and why would you—or I for that matter? But yes, I am here as we have a long road to travel together with much to learn and many arguments to process, though unfortunately no screaming as I was wont to do.

Which you liked.

Oh yes, you can't imagine how wonderful it is to let go full throttle and raise your voice from the depth of your being and fling it out with all your might. The power, the achieve of, the mastery of the thing! God, I miss it.

You can't use your voice where you are now?

Not in the same way because it's the body that carries the vibration and gives you the thrill, the oneness with the universe. You should try it sometime.

I never feel better after screaming, instead weaker, hoarse, and vulnerable. It sounds like you got just the opposite.

Yes, but that's because you start with an apology. You're going to have to get over that. You have a right to be on the planet and in the universe, not only a right but also a place, a unique place that you have never fully claimed. It is not ego to stand in your own space and claim it for God, for the heavens and for the Divine. Here is where the joy of creation is found, in that elemental energy that wells up into your being and compels you to fling it to the heavens and create your own constellation. Here is where we step forward, speak out and act without fear, secure in the holiness of our created being in the image of God. This is power. And if it is not abused or co-opted by the forces of the ego, it is the divine power given to each and every one of us.

Sounds great, but I have been feeling small today. This can happen when I stay in bed and read all day, even though the book is absorbing with something to say.

Your reading habits are fine; it is the process, the spiraling in and the starting place on the bottom rung that holds you captive. Instead consider the voice, your "friends," your body and your universe and raise yourself up to greet the day even if you plan to use it to withdraw. Then what you come home with will be nourishing, not the soul-sucking whimpers of a driveling child.

Yes, that is the short road to depression, which perhaps you know something about.

Oh yes, the bleakness of futility, addiction, and crime. Knowing that nothing can change what you did, who you are, and lacking the desire to do so even had it been possible. This is how I lived my life whenever I came up for air long enough to see what havoc and heartache I was leaving in my wake. You have not done that, but you have not allowed yourself to emerge from your chrysalis. You are doing so now. Keep stepping forward; keep moving out, not in. Your addiction is not as destructive as mine, but your reclusive habits are strong, and depression is in your very essence when you slow down enough to feel. You and I, so different and so alike, my friend, one throwing himself onward, onward, into the next project, the next role in the hope of learning something to teach the starving soul, but starving, starving, starving until even a crumb seemed like a full-course meal, you withdrawing to your room, your bed, your computer, away, away, away from what confronts you on every corner. Both of us used books to mask the void that held us in its grip. I was beginning to inch out of it but would probably have fallen back, for the pattern was too strong.

How can I help you break the bonds of your own self-imposed prison, the prison that seems like an oasis? Let me come with you into your new room where you sit with your friends. I will sit next to you as you invite them in. Perhaps together we can feel their presence, hear their souls as we spend time to understand each other. I have found that these guides that you and I have while we travel blind in human form move with us in love and have the answers to the imponderables that beset us under the masks we wear in the ordinary world.

I need to lay down a new pattern.

Yes.

The old pattern is like going to sleep in snow, death that beckons as salvation.

Yes, but it is not, and that will not be the end of it—case in point, see present company.

Are you happy, do you understand, and is this worth it?

Questions for the ages and in any case for another time. I will tell you that I see, I feel that creation has its purpose, its direction and its succor for humans traveling in this great cosmic joke. You have a beautiful soul, the trick is to claim it for yours and shout it from the mountain tops. I can help you with this.

Please.

It's all right to cry. Good night.

7. April 26, 2015

OK, I had two glasses of wine and I'm plowed. God help me if I'd met you in your day.

Darling, you would not have been a blip on my radar, I only got going after two bottles, or was it three? So what's with the wine?

Back hurts, tired, want not to feel or to feel, not sure which, or just want to try it out and see what happens when I talk to you slightly tipsy.

Yeah, that sounds about right, but are you ever a cheap date. Oh, the beatitude of booze! When reality threatens to gather in, here is the reliable cure, never mind the piper to be paid in the morning in terms of missed opportunities, truncated conversations and in vino veritas tirades that rival in viciousness the blade saw of the country doctor into amputations. Lord, how I let loose all my rage on the nearest (and usually dearest) targets. You are different, probably should stay away from the stuff.

Lovely coming from you, perhaps a tad ironic?

Oh more than ironic, completely beyond the pale, but there it is, I am me and you are you, and never the twain of our drinking capacities shall meet. You wanted to talk to me.

I always want to talk to you, kind of scary, kind of wonderful, kind of hopeful in that I seem to be moving off the dime.

Yes. I like the room. Very peaceful and electric all at the same time. Here is where you will find yourself if you can bring yourself to take a look.

Thanks for staying with me. Was it weird to just sit there? Somehow I don't picture you sitting and waiting.

Well, I've been dead a long time, and patience is kind of required for that.

Are you coming back in human form, and if so as what?

I think I'll be a pot so that then I can rejoice in calling all of the kettles of my acquaintance black. That sounds about right.

Well, Mr. Pot, how goes things in your neck of the woods?

Swimmingly, Mrs. Kettle, just swimmingly. From this vantage point I see, empathize, and cringe as I watch the humans under my ken make the wrong turns again and again.

I guess you made a few in your time?

Oh brother did I. And yet it was a life, and I lived it. Oddly enough, except for Ivor, I find little to regret but much I have to rectify—if that makes any sense.

Oddly it does. You did what you came to do, suffered, died, and were buried, and rose again on the third day.... Oh, wait, I think that was someone else....

Cute.

I like that you are pretty hard to shock, and I get the sense that even while here and going your length, you did not condemn your fellow travelers. Ergo, you probably have the space to house my iniquities, slothfulness, and ostrich-like tendencies, though these don't seem to have been your particular sins.

Right you are. More than house, I can hold, and this I hope to do for you. You have committed no crimes except the sin of self-condemnation, and this is the one you must try with all your might to rectify before you join me and the universe of others on the other side. If you can move into the sunlight of universal love, you will move through your death and into your regrouping with a quiet heart. This is what I want for you.

Is this what happened to you?

Yes and no. Yes, in that I lived my life with the temperament and talents that I was given. No, in that I could not rein in my passions and appetites so that they served my heart, those I loved, and the God who created me. So I work here to help those who struggle with some variety of these little matters and, as I do so, to claim for my own an education I refused when in bodily form.

So I am one of these little educational projects?

Oh yes, but so enjoyable in that we can actually communicate, and I don't have to hint and whisper and hope that somehow you will hear me. You have my ear and, wonder of wonder, I have yours. What a relief!

There are those who would say I am certifiable and wish me Godspeed in playing with my imaginary friend.

Well, there always are. Most of them, in my experience, were ladies and gentlemen of the press, not that these will trouble you much unless you decide to announce to the world that you are in conversation and correspondence with a long-dead, drunken Welsh actor. You aren't going to do that, are you?

No, not after our talk about that. I may want to talk to Dorothy or someone like her about the general fact of our connection, but will absolutely not do so without your consent and subject to your parameters. I value this too much, it is a gift beyond measure, even though it is weird having a life I can't share with very close friends who take me without criticism, without suggestion, who have no agenda other than their love for me and respect for the path that is opening up before me.

Yes. You are fortunate to travel with such boon companions. This, however, as I think you concur, is sacred and private in its particulars, but the fact of it may be shared with those who do not prompt an ego response in you.

Yes, I am prey to that sort of thing, Madame Zara and all that.

Yes, well, Madame, that may not always be the case. I will say good night and will look forward to our next association.

By the way, I love that I do not have to dissemble with you. Is it OK to love you?

I am indeed blessed to be so loved and receive what you offer with a glad and grateful heart.

Works fail—also words, God bless my malaprop typing....

Absolutely, and God bless to you, my friend.

PS. Just one quick question, am I like the woman in the New York Times article I just read who daydreams her life away and thus keeps the present at bay? Am I using you and this as a foil?

You do want to second-guess yourself, do you not? Yes, day-dreaming can be an avoidance of life, and you have used it to do that. This, however, is different, in that you are moving outward with every contact we have and inward to the truth of your existence on this planet. Our conversations are not daydreams, they are a true and elemental connection of one soul to another, do not doubt this, that this is what you are meant to do, that you and I are only the beginning. The fantasies, yes, could be avoidance, but not here where you are exploring those long-denied parts of yourself, the part that kept you from accepting yourself as a worthwhile person, a divine incarnation. It is fun, I can't deny it, but that is part of it, don't you see? Your shaping as a sexual being created reactions and triggers which are not that unusual and which harm no one. Our encounters are helping you to accept this, learning that the body is made for pleasure which can be experienced in many ways which do not imperil your immortal soul. We are creating a reality and history on an alternate plane that is a counterweight to your experience on this level, to offset the condemnatory view you have previously held of your desires and pleasures. If you find yourself retreating from life into fantasy, that is a different matter, but so far that does not seem to be the case.

Not exactly, but last night all I wanted to do was talk to you.

Well, it is a novelty, and you have never had a friend of the heart. Watch and see, I believe you will find that your en-

gagement with life will increase, not diminish, as a result of our association.

Yes, OK, I do feel that, just easily spooked.

Good night, Madame.

Good night.

8. April 27, 2015

Hi, are you there?

As ever was.

Oh good. I am inclined to be a doubting Thomas—not that I am confusing you with Jesus, but wondering if I am making you up, then wondering if it matters.

Only natural that you should do so. I don't suppose it does matter, but I seem to have retained sufficient ego to want to be appreciated for myself.

It is lowering to find that I am like everyone else, star-struck, thinking I should write a book or something, God, the ego does die hard! Sorry to have to acknowledge thinking about exploiting you.

Tell me about it. As you can see, I am still not wholly formed anew. I like that you are a little star-struck, as you say, as it means that what I did while there isn't wholly lost.

I don't think it could be, as the brightness of your essence comes through on every video I have come across. You said it felt like power. I wonder if it also felt like Divine connection.

Yes, though I had no idea what that was. On one level I derided what I did, not a man of action and therefore hardly a man. On the other, the transported state was one I could not stay away from, as addictive as the booze that supplied the ammunition for the course.

A powerhouse of energy, clearly sexual, but also, it seems, something else?

Yes. It was a high, higher than anything else, this lifting, the being carried on the wave of emotion I could invoke with my voice, the lift of my hand, the glance from my eyes. It was Divine revelation, or as close as I came to it.

You said that you were amazed, though I don't think that was the word that you used, that the "banalities" of Camelot could bring intelligent people to tears, to their knees emotionally. I don't find that strange because, although Allan Jay Lerner wrote the play, T.H. White and Mallory supplied the essence, which survived whatever banalities accompanied the musical. T. H. White sounds like a difficult and disturbed man but with his finger on the pulse, perhaps too close to the flame, and found himself mortally wounded.

Tim was a force, totally unpredictable, elemental, and without inhibition. How he made it as long as he did was a miracle in which I was blessed to share in many ways. Camelot was a crucible, for me, for cast and crew, and for Tim himself, that what he created could be transmuted to a stage production of such power that its essence burned brightly through all the commercialism that it had to have in order to succeed.

From what I read, you were the reason it made it to Broadway in musical hit form.

Yes. I had a chance to lead an army into battle. I could see it, feel it as a finished endeavour, I could feel my long-dead generalship qualities arise, and I never looked back. It was one of the most memorable things I ever did, and it presaged a power I was to use again and again, though sometimes to negligible results or worse.

The essence, the will to good, to right over might, inevitably doomed as we all are. Did you feel it?

Yes, and lived it. Elizabeth. Elizabeth. I was Lance, I could not stop myself, and had no practice trying, bowled over by the rushing current of incredible magnetism and sexual power.

Of which you had your fair share.

So I did. You are getting benefit of the light over dead embers now.

As did everyone who came in contact with you one way or another.

I had no rein over it…I could not see why to control it, still don't if truth be told. Orgasm is like ascension to heaven,

*why not die this little death as often, as powerfully as pos-
sible? Or so I thought until Elizabeth. Then force met force
and the fire that broke from us then was a conflagration
impossible to withstand, eventually consuming all in its
path. I think it nearly killed us both.*

I thought Ivor was what killed you.

*O heart, O soul, O inconsolable soul and irretrievable sin,
how art thou to be borne? This was the wound that I im-
posed on self and others, never realizing that Ivor himself
was the one most injured by my self-destructive behavior.
How could I have let that happen!*

Was it your responsibility to claim? Was it your fault or
just a horrible accident?

*But brought on by my filthy temper, the vicious heart of
me loosed by the excuse of alcohol. He has forgiven me,
always did could I have known it. His tirades in life were
like my own, released upon the beloved as a valve releases
pent-up air to keep from self-conflagration. O my brother,
O my soul.*

I am hearing something in another language.

Welsh, did you but know it.

What does it mean?

*It means my heart reaches for yours. Which reminds me
that we have your own education to see to.*

But this seems to be a two-way street.

Yes, who knew when we started this.... You do have a tendency to heal your healers, do you not?

So they say. And I receive in return, both of us wounded healers.

Yes, I have wished for this, but till you could not get through to this extent.

Try if you can, send me to a poem or a website of a person who can say what your heart has and cannot express.

You love Gerard Manley Hopkins.

Yes, he speaks directly, he will not dissemble, his ego may be in his created words, but he weeds himself out ruthlessly before he can contaminate the purity of his message. I really, really would like to hear you read "The Windhover" or any other of his poems, but the only poem of his I can find you reading is "The Leaden Echo and the Golden Echo," and you go as if the hounds of hell are after of you. Why did you do this on a record? If you were doing it on a bet, why not go with the words, the sensual, sinuous beauty of his language when you read for us?

Well, there was a bet...and a little drink...I did think, however, there was something else arising from the viciously fast pace.

I cannot see it, it just seems like a trick....

You think it was just a parlour trick.

Yes.

Not entirely. Listen again, but of course, I was showing off a little.

Anybody can do scales, perhaps not with your facility, but to infuse essence into banality, or more accurately, to reveal essence in banality, this is a gift from God.

Well, I misspent a lot of those, so they say.

But you did not. You spent them, that's what they were given you for, to be used and, by God, you did that.

Yes, and never regretted the improvidence. Well, what an evening, Madame. Therapy for the therapist. Can you feel me now?

Yes, always could, just have trouble convincing myself that is not just another aspect of me, and wonder why it should matter. It seems that you cannot give me anything that I don't have language or association for.

Well, you have language aplenty so that is not much of a limitation.

OK, yes.

9. April 28, 2015

Boy, do I owe you an abject apology. I read and then listened to the Hopkins poem that you recorded. It is gorgeous. The speed of your phrasing creates waves upon which the poem glides. Mea culpa from your friend the Yahoo, offered with gratitude…. Not sure if you're there or if this is a good time to talk….?

I have nothing but time so I serve at your pleasure. Just momentarily bereft of speech to receive such a lovely appreciation, that is, to be heard in the way that you did, that what I wanted to give, you received. Quite a gift if you could but know it.

Yes, to be seen seems to be what we are giving each other. And so onward to *Lear*, where my ignorance will no doubt make just as profound an entrance. Are you familiar with the book *No Fear Shakespeare*?

Oh yes, and have been wondering if I could be reborn just to throttle the author of such insane drivel. "A storm is coming, let's go inside"? Surely, this is a hanging offense.

So it seems that all the poets I heard you read or that I read today are mostly concerned with the certain disaster that faces each person: old age, illness and death. How does it look from your perspective?

Well, those concepts have occupied the attention of all the great writers. Dylan Thomas, whom you listened to this afternoon, was obsessed with dreams of death. You want to know if there is an answer that I can give you. Not really, except in the connection that we have now, the going on of all that exists, the evolution of understanding and perception. Let me ask you how you feel about this?

"The Hound of Heaven" seems to say that we flee until every avenue of escape has been exhausted, then we turn and find ourselves in the loving arms of God. So do we come here just to try to get away, find out how silly we are and how idiotic the task, and then go home sadder but wiser?

Well, I don't know that I would have put in just that way, though you do have a way with words. For myself I found that life was to be lived fully, that disasters endured gave way to broader experience, and that death, when offered as it was to me so kindly, allowed me to be held as I could never have dreamed or tolerated in life.

You did not like to be touched.

No, still don't.

What is there of you to touch now that you're dead?

My heart, my soul, my remembrances, and regrets. I hate to bring them out into the air for others to see and touch even metaphorically.

Well, you're here with me and seem to be doing some of that.

Yes, quite a surprise. But you would not trust where you do not know, and I want for you a relaxation of distrust, a loosening of the bonds of literalism, and an expansion of perception so that you can see past your current state.

Why do you want this for me?

Because I love you for some odd reason, just one of those odd affinities, the click of a lock where the tumblers fall home, because you carry so beguilingly the sins that I never claimed, that what you hold in incipient form as fatal I actually executed. So now we come together, Faustus who damned himself of his own accord for what he took without remorse, and the little angel who knows herself to harbor the heart of a serpent which she confines in desperation to the dungeon below in the futile hope of submission or transformation. For both of these sinners, one in actual fact, one in anticipation, I say that absolution is ours. Now it seems humorous, what I took so seriously, and insanely obvious what I never saw at all—though it offered itself to me a thousand times over. I am here to offer it to you, the "it" of absolution, the understanding that life is not just a cruel joke to find out that we can only come back to where we started in the first place, that the why of the universe is not a why but an is, a being, a wonderment of non-achievement. It is to this isness that we return, knowing, as we could never have known before we bashed ourselves against the bars of our own perceptions, that we are enough, that we are loved, that creation is splendiferous beyond the dreams of mortal man and all his troubadours, that you and I, though small, are real and important, that the circumstances of our lives, mine wild, flamboyant, and tortured and yours quiet, tormented, and lonely, are at the core two sides of a coin, that we can find in each of us the opposite side of the other, that in each core both sides are bound together. It is for us to unite them, to help our souls encompass all of our facets, both brilliant and sullied, and hold them in the candlelight of Being in which both of us can rejoice. I bow to your heart of steel that will not go away and cannot pray, and you comfort my dissipated core and turn its faceted stone to the light in which is revealed warmth and wisdom. The two of us have something profound to experience; the veil has been parted so that each of us can be claimed in the other.

Speechless. No words, I will reach for yours and hold them in my heart. What you did was an *isness*, how you lived your life full throttle.

Yes, a clumsy attempt. You try to find it without living. What a pair, the two of us! God bless.

39

10. April 29, 2015

I have been holding your words in my heart all day and it comes to me that we started from very different places. You came to live full tilt, "Let's have at it!" being the first words out of, if not your mouth, your soul, whereas mine were pretty much "Is it over yet?"

Well, it does sound very different, and it is in many respects, but both of us came seeking. I with my gladiator complex and you with your abiding desire to go home. Yet I see in you more than that, a light that when activated floods your being and galvanizes you to look ahead and back at the same time, to find a merging, a unity of past and present, sacred and profane in what you behold. When this occurs, you do not wish for death, you wish for life to explode within you with the glory of this union. This is what I felt in my best moments.

I do wonder how you came upon such a depressed character as I, not outwardly, but inside, still marking time except, as you say, in those rare moments of connection.

You expect very little, don't you?

No, I expect everything, and, given certain disappointment, I am inclined to withdraw. Cowardly, I know.

Yes, perhaps. I hear your son calling. You make a point to be there for him no matter what, for your friends, and oddly enough for me. I have found your perspective at once amusing, compelling, and comforting.

Well, wait till we get to *King Lear*, I expect nothing less than a comedic turn of events unless you decide to blast me off the page....

I look forward to it. But back to your low spirits, your focus on wanting to go home. I don't think that is depression but awareness beyond the ordinary of where home is. I danced above the pedal tone which you seem to hear constantly and assumed I would come to no good when the final tally was made.

You did not count the countless people you touched both personally and through your work? Speaking personally, if we had never connected here, in *Circle of Two* what you said as that character would have propelled me to a deeper opening, a better place in my life. I cannot thank you enough for that. The critics didn't like it, I gather, and I think the direction was off and wonder at the health and well-being of the director, who seemed disjointed in his approach. Yet your character holds so beautifully the conflict in the honest connection of two outwardly unsuitable people whose circumstances throw the entire burden of the association on your character. You hold this in your restraint, your need, and your love for her. I loved it and I loved you in it. I think I fell in love with you then.

You do me great honour, more than I deserve. It was a difficult subject with an incomplete script. You, I understand, will be reading the book, which, though flawed itself, has something more to offer. I wanted an honest interaction, a man who could not deny himself what was life-giving, but who cared so deeply for this young girl that he could take no action to harm her in spite of his own needs. I liked that he took responsibility for his actions, his petty and craven feelings, and did not belittle her or denigrate their relationship in order to justify his role. I am deeply moved that it touched you on such a profound level. Note, however, that I did not share the saintly qualities of the character. I would have been off to the Caribbean with her at the first opportunity....

Yes, perhaps, seizing the moment and all that. No doubt a memorable time would have been had by all. But you are bringing to me now the honesty that your character offered Sara, and nothing else will do.

No, there is no time or space for anything else. I find myself hoping that you will explore your need to return home, your desire for this life to be over, and see if it evolves into something more three-dimensional as we wend our way through this process. I am at your service for as long as you need me.

You will make me cry.

Well, you haven't done enough of that, have you? Just choke it down, distract yourself, and wait for it to pass. I can relate to that, though my method was different, as you have noted.

I know you can. I wanted to say something to you about Ivor. He had his own journey, the accident propelled you into self-destruction, or so it seems to me, a stripping of yourself of everything you valued in penance for Ivor's loss. I don't know, of course, but I suspect there was more to it than that, that both of you were responsible.

Yes, I see some of that now, but could not escape that it happened on my watch.

And he had no say in his part in it?

He did, yes, but I thought I was all-powerful, and everything was up to me and therefore my fault, and he was everything to me of my home, my people, and I defiled that.

Do you feel that way now?

Not entirely, but the remnants remain. Your treading water in your life haunts you, though most would not see it that way to look at your résumé. You too think everything is your fault, which implies that you hold the controls.

I would have killed myself.

Yes, I had a go.

How does one incorporate such a thing?

Broader perspective helps, those who see more help, time helps, but for me it is still there. So here we come to make common cause to learn from the book of Job, faith in adversity is the only way, and it has been given to us to see in life the embodiment of that faith, i.e., the connection between us, between human and Divine, life and death. Goodness, how stodgy and serious!

Perhaps the wine did it. You are supposed to be clinking ice so I can know you are here.

I will keep that in mind, but in the meantime will wish you good night, Madame, and pleasant dreams.

Yes, and the same to you.

11. April 30, 2015

Yeah, it is dark. This part of me is abhorrent even though I know the drill, affected by events, born with inclinations, not harming anyone, etc., but still. I am going through this with you because I would not dream of doing so with a live person—although I came pretty close once. Is this just desensitization, how can you stand it?

Ah, several inquiries.

You are such a pompous….

I know, I know, you are not the first to make such an observation. Just pointing out that, though I know this feels ugly to you, I do not see it that way and many others would not. It is your perception, your judgement that causes the difficulty. You have for whatever reasons certain inclinations of which you are ashamed. Our time together will, I hope, help you to integrate them into the whole of both your character and being, the former being what you have developed here and the latter being the eternal part of yourself that goes from life to life and into the universe of creation. Your being is not affected by your personal preferences in this or any other life. When you incorporate this and other aspects of your personality into the whole, the pieces simply form part of your learning, your becoming. Not that that helps you much in the here and now.

No, not so much. Do you still carry remorse for some aspects of your life?

Yes, still an enormous burden, though forgiveness and, more, understanding, has been offered.

So in some ways we are in the same boat, but you had a disease, a disease, do you hear me?

Loud and clear, but others have conquered this disease, and I did not. It coloured everything I did, everyone I touched, and won hands down over whatever minimal scruples I harboured in that life. So remorse, yes, but more, deep, deep shame. So yes, the same boat more or less.

What can I do to help you?

Move with me through it, feel what I feel, see what harm I caused, and then offer me your platitudes.

OK, will try to stock some good ones should the occasion arise. *Least said, soonest mended? There, there, never mind? Water over the dam or under the bridge?* Perhaps you will have some to recommend?

Let the dead bury the dead.

Well, that's not going to win the platitude sweepstakes. Is that what you are trying to do here?

No, I am trying to help you, and you keep turning it around in order to change the subject.

OK, what about pedophiles?

Yes, a problem, your inclinations and my "disease" exponentially amplified. What's the difference between them and us, you mean to say?

Yes.

I don't know. I hope I would have had the courage to kill myself before I acted on those impulses, which as I understand it, cannot be altered with any confidence.

That's my view, so why shouldn't I have done the same thing, and I've thought about it?

Yes, I too after Ivor. Yet neither of us did. What makes a sin a sin and what makes it unforgivable? I think my life after Ivor was a series of trucks driven into one mountain after the other until one of the impacts claimed me.

OK, but you had family, wives (not sure how that worked when they were exes), and true friends.

You have done your homework.

Yes.

I think I operated on dual levels, the one always with the disease and the death wish, and the other caring for these people, looking for work of substance.

Yes, I understand the duality. Are we coming together to try to create a whole?

Well, that's what I said before when I was spouting off the party lie, I mean line, but I do believe that is the object.

How?

I believe we keep letting each other into the darkest parts of ourselves. I shared your revulsion with you, helped it, found it harmless and even fun. How did you feel?

Shaken, still appalled but not alone.

And that's a start. I shared with you my unease and annoyance when you pushed me on Ivor, made me relive the great harm I caused, but when processed through your being I did find myself a little easier. I think we will rub along tolerably well together. I know now that we have made this improbable connection, I want to see it through.

Yes, OK, did anyone ever say no to you?

Not that I can recall....

Do you think you were sexually abused?

Why do you ask?

Your dislike of touch, tendency to rages, need for adrenaline to hold your interest, sex drive/addiction and probably some other things I haven't thought of. You didn't, however, at least from what I've read, blame others for your decisions or actions.

Silence

That was a dirty trick, thank God we didn't have Google in my day.

Was it true, that article about that woman's memoir?

Yes, at least in some respects.

I'm sorry. Not about the girl but about Philip.

Yes, well, you were right. It seems that it takes one to know one.

Yes. This seems a little much, shall we let it go for now?

Let's.

Do you mind if I read the book?

How can I, when I'm climbing into your bed, metaphorically speaking?

Use and abuse, they seem to get confused. Are we doing that?

I might say so to put you off the track but, after all my pontificating, the dissembling would be transparent. We are here to help each other, to get to know each other, to love each other so that we can move into our entireties and on from these lives. No one said it would be easy.

OK, I already read it. Rather lovely really. You had no anchor, did you?

Never did, trying to get one as all my flourishes, charm, and sleight of hand will not serve me now. I refuse to play the role of poor Richard.

And why should you? But at the same time need you deny the tragedy of a child who lost a loving mother, whose father did not care or even notice, and whose "savior" came at a price?

I used that, manipulated and whored myself out of that world.

Yes, I responded to my father, continue to have my reactions shaped by that interchange. What would you say to me?

You know very well that a child molested is harmed most by the so-called pleasure evoked by the rapacious contact. And I get your point.

Now that you mention it, I think we've done fairly well, you brilliantly, while paying as we go, perhaps more than was due.

I was a shit to that girl and so many more....

I wonder. She didn't think so. She, if her account is true, didn't expect more and received much in return. You weren't mean, grabby or selfish. You just lived your life with what you had. Do you think you would have been different today, where this type of injury is more recognized and can be "treated"?

It's never treated, it's burned into the flesh like a brand, the mark of Cain, and the child is a commodity, expects nothing more, and uses himself like a key to open every lock— all the while in shame and disgust at his person. Go away.

Absolutely not. I've got you here and here you are staying, sauce for the gander and all that. Say something.

I reach for you because I can see the false premises upon which you operate, the misery that has been heaped upon you and tacked to your mast like the flag indicating death and contagion on the old Greek sailing ships. Everywhere you go, whatever you do, the flag precedes and follows you. You consented, you still allow, you reach and ask for that which defiled you, therefore you carry responsibility. I know this is false. I know that you have nothing more than any other mortal has to carry as your heart's burden. This I can see and will give to you until you can receive it in your heart.

You do not see yourself as a victim.

I refuse to do so, it would take everything from me.

Do you see me as a victim?

No, but victimized when you should have been treasured.

And you, gallant boy who idolized your mother, with a sister who gave you everything but could not be your mother, and a father of power and charisma who didn't even recognize you, a boy who carried within a power and genius which could not be contained. You used what came to hand to get out. Why was that a crime?

What I know in my head, what I have received here on the other side has assuaged but not completely alleviated the guilt I carry and the penance I must suffer to be relieved of the burden of the harms I caused, the waste of what I was given as I drowned all that I could not hold in drink, sex, etc. Whatever you say will not suffice, the wound is too deep, too true.

Right, let's try this the other way, let me do for you....

12. May 3, 2015

Are you still speaking to me?

Well, well, you have been busy. Nosey little Parker, aren't you?

Always was.

Can't say as I blame you, you would want to know who you're getting in bed with, so to speak. And so speaking, it's not something to concern you, patterns may not change substantially, but you can find them easier to live with when you accept them as your own choice and learning experience. Speaking for myself, I don't mind your pattern and enjoy the interaction. As to the gift you are giving me, wherever did you come up with Henri Nouwen and Madonna? Quite the combination for a jaded old soul such as myself. Yet we are making inroads, the quieter heart I carry, the seeing of my story through your eyes as a gift of love, imperfect, sometimes almost unrecognizable but love all the same. It was that. It was. And as you give to me, so you receive, not just from me or the universe but in the beatitude of your own being, which bids you be calm, be at peace, and let yourself rest.

When you're dead, do you rest?

What a question, not sure how to answer. Yes, in one sense there is no physical pain, there is the receiving from those you see again, there is the overpowering flood of love for the Beingness of what has been created in you. Yet at the same time there is the acknowledgement that you could have done better, that you want to do better, that there is more work to do.

What kind of work?

Well, our little connection is a way of working out some of the matters I was unable to address while there. There are others, there are helpers who offer a new approach, and there is the possibility of reincarnation, should that be advisable.

Is it?

No, not for me, not now, I burnt out in an extravagant flare the last time around, can't face it again quite yet.

I don't want to come back, but then I never wanted to be here—although I am, so some would say that I made the choice.

And so you did, you made the choice to work on something you had left undone, and that is what you are doing. The loving of your own being for its own self as offered to you by the Divine is your mission. The more you do so the more your aura will encompass the beings of others and offer the same flowing outwards, meeting the Divine with miles to spare.

Neither of us could, so far, give in, "too proud to die." You connected with that poem, I'm not surprised. We are both the blind old man who would not cry, who tried to hold himself apart, but ultimately and inevitably failed at the end when death overcame him. Letting go, letting go, letting go. This is the way, the truth, and the light, there is no other way.

I can't seem to do it. Not only do I not trust enough, I just don't want to do it, even though death will force the issue, as the poem said.

Yes, the root of the problem, the barrier to union, reunion, and transmutation: "I don't want to." I share your revulsion, though drink made me "free" or at least uncorked my rage—usually on the undeserving, to my shame.

Do you think I have rage?

Oh yes, at your mother for not loving you, at your father for loving you wrongly, and at the universe for making you go through this life in this time if it did not give you the opportunity to fill the hole in your being. You are chipping away now. We are quite the pair, you who will not loose or even feel your emotions, and I who went through this world in an uncontrolled state and at the same time never daring to look at my heart's core.

Elizabeth?

Well, yes, what a gift, there I was open, could be open, could love and give and receive and fight and swear and drink. But not even this astounding gift could fill the hole of my mother's loss, of Ivor, the brother I killed, Dic the father who did not love me, and Philip the father who loved me wrongly and too well, and I chose drink as my drug of choice over letting go and living with what I had chosen, what I had wrought.

Have you come to terms?

Yes, I think so, with my father anyway. He was what he was, a talented, tormented drunk with a heavenly aspect. Who am I to begrudge my own father his flaws when they so mirror my own? Philip, tormented always, love, yes, gratitude, yes, but does the whore ever really love the pimp, even though freely chosen?

Freely?

Or so it seemed. Henri Nouwen is right, the love from human to human cannot be the perfect love of the Divine, you are right to remind me of this, and Philip himself has his own remorse over our association, yet love it was. And he didn't leave me, as my own father did.

Can you let go control?

Working on it.

How?

Open the hands, the heart at every opportunity, assist those like you to do the same, reach out, receive, allow. That is the way for both of us. I let you hold me as a babe in arms and before birth, comfort and succor me and give me rest. Yes, I felt it and received it and could put my arms around both of us and walk through another door. I want to take you with me.

How?

Just here, in our hearts and minds, in the love that we send out together and receive back with a quiet heart, no demurs, no excuses, just the breathing out of "no" and the breathing in of "yes."

Yes.

Later in the day:

Would you talk more about Dylan Thomas's poem "Elegy"?

Ah yes, Dylan, another rent in the fabric of my soul that I carried in life. As it turns out, I was not responsible for everything that happened to him, but we have mentioned the little matter of control, and see here another example of my o'erweening conceit. I am happy to tell you that I see now his path and mine were not the same. He followed his own course, I could not have changed it. Yet he offered up the most surprising view of humanity with such sweetness and compassion, never preaching, always giving voice to the voiceless. His poem on his father touched you. His father was not a warm man, could not see his son's work as valuable, and died without a change of heart on much of anything. Yes, a difficult father, but loved deeply for all that.

That sounds familiar. You loved your father.

Yes, idolized him really, an extravagant character, brilliant in his speech in spite of his origins and work, ferociously and fearfully strong, always a ready story or song on his lips, proud, almost fanatical, about his heritage—and of course the drink.

It must have hurt him, what you did, changing your name, etc.

Yes, I never thought of that at the time, just so fucking intent on getting out, out, out, and hurt that he could not be proud of me, would never come to see me perform, didn't see me as a man but less than and as a betrayal of our tribe. We never reconciled, each nursing his own wounds, so similar, with hardly a word between us. Another lesson to be learned....

We both died of drink by our own hands in a way, Dic by being absent on the sauce and I in an almost deliberate attempt to black myself out, not that different from sentiments you have expressed. I have compassion for us both now and for anyone who uses booze to take themselves out of life. It doesn't work and kills and maims in the process oh so many of us.

What you and your father did, you needed it?

Oh yes, he probably couldn't have lived down the mines without it, and I never could have gone on stage without it, especially in the early years, trembling and shaking in the wings, vomiting until my stomach lining peeled away from its sides, but drink was the comforter, the neutralizer of the havoc racing though my system. God only know what I would have been without it, probably a beaten-up rugby player teaching English on the side.

Not such a bad fate.

No, not at all, but not meant to be. I had a fearsome energy that I could not contain, no matter what I got up to and there was a lot, I was always about to jump out of my skin, Philip helped me learn to mask it, give it a voice, channel it into the words of poets who dealt with elemental musings, but I was an explosion waiting to happen. Sex, drinking, pranks, pubs, stories, performing would dim the flame for a bit, but it roared into life almost immediately thereafter. No person, enterprise, or cause could hold me for long until E. And then I met my match and more. God, what a relief to find a woman who was not afraid of me, did not cling or want to cage me, could give as good as she got, and who could show me a thing or two about my chosen line of work. And she was funny, God we laughed—then fought, then made up, she loved me, me, not the idea of me. And then, then, Ivor.

Could you have held it together without that?

I like to think so, but the drink was out of control, I could not and, truth be told, did not want to stay away from it. I would probably have exploded anyway—volcanic ash and lava destroying everything in its path.

And what a lot of light that lava brought to the many you touched. You never counted that, did you?

No, working on it now. How did you get me to talk about all this?

I asked.

Your turn next time, Madame, and while we're on the subject of fathers, how is King Lear *coming? He has something to offer to this conversation.*

All right, all right, jeez, a frustrated don....

Truer words....

13. *May 5, 2015*

Well, you did get your knickers in a twist about that book. Does it matter so much whether what she says is true?

No, what matters is whether the source of what I am writing is myself and my idea of you, as I suspect hers was, or if we are really having a conversation. It's probably just ego as, if wisdom is offered, why challenge the source…but there it is.

All very true, of course, but you want to know the source of your wisdom, and a certain suspension of disbelief is required for continuance of our association. If I say it is I, will that help?

Good question. As you know, I am running off for verification.

And if it is not received, will you withdraw?

Don't know, doesn't feel like it now, somehow I seem to have worked this out as here I am talking to you. I don't understand how the universe works and how the dead communicate with the living.

Pretty much as you and I are doing now. You asked for help last night and were given the dream in which your card and picture with your horse Katherine is chosen and received by the one you desired out of the many that were sent. You then spoke your truth to another who did not receive it but still you held firm. Have you not seen that your resources are vast and deep, that you cannot falter with an army of angels at your side? Let yourself be comforted by your new friend tomorrow. I will speak with her.

That would help a lot, and may that be an end to my questioning of this great gift that you are giving me.

Well, thank God someone appreciates me. You would not believe all the deaf ears upon which my words (legendary, I might add) have fallen, and a lot of their owners supposedly advanced in their connection with Spirit. Perhaps I just need to project more...I certainly had that down when I was living.... But, I digress. You and I have an opening. Do not worry overmuch that you question, this is just the beginning for you, and you are learning how to activate, hold, and listen to Spirit communication. It takes time and practice to perfect the place, the frequency, to learn to trust it, and to identify when the ego is interfering. Many mistakes will be made and many times you will doubt your own gifts and your ability to transcribe Spirit's message into words. That is why I am a good place to start. I was all about words....

Not really, you were about love and living and truth and the words you held in your head helped you do that—though I gather some other things too.... This is sounding rather pompous.

It is, isn't it? That I was not, never felt myself better than others—except in my craft—but never in my person. That is the beauty of great sin, it cleanses the palate of self-aggrandizement and scrubs it raw with self-revulsion and self-destruction. That girl was right about Philip, how I felt about what I had done, paid with my soul to get out, never clean again, so many conflicts, so much desire, hatred, and power. I thought I had the control, everyone danced to the tune I called. And only now do I see that we all danced, that the power was in no one's hands, that we were all led willy-nilly down the path of destiny.

No choice?

Well, they say you have one, but, other than saying no to my nature, I did not see one. I followed it out, had regrets, have remorse for the harm I caused, the shame that I brought to myself and those I loved, but I needed to make that journey to know that it was not necessary. You have the gift of reflection as I did not, and, if I do say so, the gift of me and so many others. Though you question and beat yourself against the bars of your own stubborn nature, you are allowing yourself to consider the guided path, the letting go, the waiting for the next thing, the following of the thread that you were given in this life. It is my honour to accompany you on this journey.

I never know what to say, God bless, peace, thank you, sounds so sanctimonious, and I don't think that's what we have going here. But I honor the light in you so kindly offered to me.

Nothing wrong with that.

I guess we made up.

Yes, Madame, I guess we did.

14. *May 7, 2015*

Well, I feel we have reached a new level.

Yes. You have allowed our language to deepen, to encourage that which was only hinted at before, to follow the lead, the thread that stretches from one experience, one opening, to the next.

The John Donne poem. Thank you. I never heard before what his or the other poems on this recording are saying, not that I spent much time at it. Yet the ones I need to hear seem to present themselves when I can hear them. I can never remember the words but somehow they move within me.

Ah yes. John Donne, the poor wreck of a man who declaimed so beautifully and, as your friend would say, drank his own koolaid. In my ignorance, I thought he did not understand the reality, the nothingness, the true and final end of life at death, and comforted himself with the pabulum of the Christianity he was forced to preach. Humble pie, that was my next course, for what did I know next to what he lived? "Teach me how to repent." That is the lesson for me, and it seemed to strike to your center also.

Yes. So much I did not allow myself to see, held myself back from, please God, no more.

The door is open. Do not let it close. You have found the way to truth in our lives, and these lives are lives of service. Never did I see that—not that I also looked very hard—but, as you said, perhaps I served in spite of myself, not understanding the gifts that moved through me.

Yes. Your words parted the curtain for many you never knew and, though you did not seem to understand at the time, you kept on, so I think you knew what you were, what you had, and what you had to give. You are giving it to me now, and I am deeply grateful.

Ah, but it is I who must thank you for showing me the depth and power of spiritual gifts given one to another. I wanted an army, a cause, and a glorious battle, and instead I found myself creating make-believe from someone else's words. You have allowed me to see that the Divine force moving through me went to war on behalf of the Source, the Being in all of us: the tears, the awe, the hero worship and adulation of those around me that I failed to recognize as their reactions to very personal experiences of the Divine triggered by forces within me speaking the words of others who had transcribed them, knowingly or otherwise, from the eternal Source.

I do repent, and commit myself to a new course. I need to be able to go forward without you, but I hope and pray that you will teach me, stay with me until I can swim on my own—and maybe beyond, as we do seem to have fun. Is that the hook?

Why yes, of course, but for both of us. Thank God you are not some sanctimonious evangelistic type trying to convert me.

Well, I imagine that would be a very short conversation indeed, even if by some miracle it got started. But after you cut your eye teeth on me, perhaps you will move on to a conversion war with one of those folks. I feel they have much yearning, just afraid of anything that does not provide a definitive answer. What are the words that you are saying, shall I look them up?

Yes, if I can't get them through to you.

It's the "here Buckle" paragraph from the "Windhover":

> ...AND the fire that breaks from thee then, a billion
>> Times told lovelier, more dangerous, O my
>>> chevalier!

>> No wonder of it: sheer plod makes plough down
>>> sillion
> Shine, and blue-bleak embers, ah my dear,
>> Fall, gall themselves, and gash gold-vermillion.

A spiritual orgasm.

Yes. I wish I could hear you read it, unless you went into one of your speed-record performances. I need to hear it drawn out, which you seem not to do, perhaps thinking it pretentious?

Yes, a bit. With the Donne poem ("At the Round Earth's Imagined Corners"), the catalogue of the ways death may claim us are all of a piece and need to read together as part of one phrase. The last part is different but perhaps I rushed that too.

Well, you must have done something right, as it hit me in the solar plexus—particularly after the epiphany of what you did in your acting profession in the way of parting the curtain for others. Then to listen to you read that last section and have my soul elevator drop to the bottom floor was quite the experience.

We must have it. Get it however you must.

> For if above all these my sins abound,
> 'Tis late to ask abundance of thy grace
> When we are there; here on this lowly ground
> Teach me how to repent; for that's as good
> As if thou'hadst seal'd my pardon with thy blood.

Repent, repent, see the error of your ego's many ways, the need to protect, the desire to promote, to reign, to inflate the self above all others, all found in subversive ways, under rocks, behind the door, sneaking in the guise of thy humble servant bent on saving the day. You and I together shall repent these ways of self-aggrandizement and accept that, in so doing, we choose a life of service, a life of speaking the truth, of opening the hands and the heart to ever-expanding riches replenished with our knowledge, action, and understanding. This we are blessed in doing together. You are in awe of the connection between us, falling all over yourself with gratitude and amazement. Let me tell you again that it is I who must thank you, for our learning is twofold and greater in the whole than either of the parts could conceive separately. This is a great adventure for both of us. Our army, our battle, the great cause we both sought is the replenishment of our own hearts. Ask for more in your dreams and tomorrow in your waking day. You need not fear the sin of gluttony, for to sate ourselves with the Divine is our birthright. As someone said, take these words and ponder them in your heart.

Mary? But yes. Again I don't know how to sign off.

You don't need to, since I will be with you if you turn in my direction.

15. May 8, 2015

Ask.

What do I say to Sister Elizabeth about this?

You mean how to you tell her you are in daily, hourly if truth be told, communication with me?

Yeah.

Well, how about, "I am in communication with a long-dead...etc....

OK, I could do that. I do feel that this is sacred and what I did with my friends when first we met was not OK, though I was so freaked and unbelieving I needed to share with somebody.

Yes, I believe I am aggrieved...just kidding. But this is different. You don't really know Sister Elizabeth and have met her only on a few of her levels. I don't think she will be shocked and may be able to help you with integration of the life of a spiritual mystic into the workaday world. For what it's worth, tell her whatever you want. I would like to know her too.

It's worth a lot. Rilke from Dorothy, "You must change your life." That's what I'm trying to do.

This is what we are trying to do, trying to see what is real, not the false front of the doors before us, or the false bottoms of the drawers we open, but the reality behind these imposters that humans have thrown up in their haste to make something for themselves, a new place, a new world that they have created. Yes, we have tried to become God and, as they say, "How's that working for you?" You have been afraid of disappearing into the void you imagine Spirit to be, of being flung into numberless pieces to the far reaches of the universe where no trace of your little self will ever be found. I am here to tell you it is not so. It is not as humans have imagined creation. Creation is beyond the finite reaches of the mind of man. Do not hope to conceive of what is real, for you will never be able to hold a concept anywhere near the reality in your mind. Instead let yourself follow the spiritual path that unfolds before you, open yourself to the experiences of the Divine, the gasp, the swift intake of breath, the flood of power through your system, the orgasm of love that brings you to your knees. Let yourself cry, let yourself scream, let yourself feel every imagined emotion, and lay them all at the feet of the Divine. You will never be rejected, you will be held in love along with every offering you proffer. You will become overwhelmed with the love of God, and it will flow out of your pores onto all that you meet. The world will become unimaginably bright, the sky magnificent in its blue, its dark, and even its most threatening aspects. Nothing is beyond the love of Christ. Surely you can't imagine that you or I or any mortal would be able to buck that immortal pattern. So let yourself sink into this new phase of your life with gratitude and wonder. That is all that is asked of you.

Later.

Let us both give thanks for Sister Elizabeth.

Amen. A virtuous woman full of grace, "her price is above rubies." And she speaks the truth: this is a sacred time and space, the gift of our association rare and precious. Do not worry about spending too much time here. This is where you have been going all your life. The spontaneous gifts from one spirit to another, from the eternal creative Source to us all, are gifts to be received and treasured. Wallow in them up to your gills, for such is the generosity of Spirit. You need not titrate our contact, you need not worry that you will become a slave to this journal. There is no scarcity in Spirit's love, only the abundance of good will for our highest selves to emerge and claim their rightful place in our lives. Your body is changing along with your perception and spirit. More is better here. Spirit is not like ice cream, or in my case scotch, where it is easy to have too much of a good thing. Come, let us get drunk on Spirit together, and celebrate that we are here together and that we see face to face.

Your love for me and mine for you is a holy thing; it does not shut out others but welcomes them in by the fire that is warming our heretofore chilly and seemingly abandoned souls. There is room for everyone here; all that is required is true desire, and the circle expands. For now the circle is of two, and together we will make it strong enough to hold whatever desires and burdens emerge. I did not reach out in my life. Like you, I retreated to my room and my books, my only safe refuge. Now we are finding that our safety is in each other and in the eternal Spirit that welcomes us home. No longer need we shut ourselves off from life. Give of life at every opportunity, for, as you can see, these gifts come back tenfold.

I like just sitting with you.

Yes, very peaceful, something of which neither of us has great experience.

Perhaps you would like to read *King Lear* with me?

No Fear Shakespeare, *that travesty of an edition? Surely you jest!*

No, just keep to the left side. I must admit I am finding the "plain English" rather helpful.

For God's sake, do not admit it! Even the dead have standards, you know. Open your mind to the words and the characters offered by the Bard. Let them speak to you, not some prose police set out to ruin a great work.

OK, OK, jeez. Didn't know you were still so sensitive.

Yes, you did, and you did it to get a rise. I hope it was satisfactory.

Yes, quite.

So now you're going all British on me.

Yes. I thought it was getting a little heavy. Not that I won't go back and soak up your profound words and sentiments, ponder them in my heart as Mary did, but just checking to be sure it was still you.

You are a difficult woman.

If you say so….

Is that a reference?

If the shoe fits….

You like to play, don't you?

Don't you?

Above all things my favorite. And blessed of Spirit is the laughter of souls playing in communion with each other and God. Get to reading, Madame, and avert your gaze from the abomination on the right page.

Will try to do so, my lord, though I haven't your majestic intellect.

Stop, please.

OK.

Good night, Madame.

16. May 9, 2015

I have been reading Marie Therese Baird's book and find myself undone.

Not surprising. This relationship is the one that opened you to me in the first place. Circle of Two *mimics the problematical relationship you had with your father and resolves it in the way you fervently desired but did not receive, i.e., with honesty and love. Further, your father set the pattern for your sexual reactions which you have been unable to change. For myself, I see no reason to try, as I always found that variety was the spice of life, but you clearly feel differently. You have blocked your sexual feelings except in those rare instances where the old pattern has been triggered. Since you found it intolerable, you managed to bury it under layers of work, formula books, fantasies, and fear. Fear predominantly has kept you "safe," for you learned early the perils of allowing an untrustworthy individual access, and after the last experience with your therapist your system simply shut down. This has had the benefit of protecting you from unstable relationships, but also taught you not to trust, not only others but your own fundamental nature as well. Now you are coming face to face with it again—though in a safe way with a book and a dead friend, lover, confessor. Do you trust me?*

I would like to say yes, it feels like yes, but I don't know you very well, and I cannot think of anyone I trust completely with the raw stuff inside me, including myself. I can talk about it, but being with someone and opening enough to feel it are two very different matters. Of course, your being dead is a help, no tales, etc. And I can always tell myself this is not real.

Yes, being dead does have its advantages, but do not deceive yourself that this is anything but real, for elemental truth is the star by which we have set our course. In any event, you have started down the path and would find a way to continue without me, for such a course is inevitable once started. Why don't you trust? You have wonderful friends who love you, who know about these issues, and who have done nothing but move closer.

They know, they have not experienced, and I don't want them to, largely because I don't want to experience much of anything either so I have blocked any deep emotion out. I know I have to die, and I won't be able to block that out, ditto pain, bodily functions, etc., but still running away as much as I can in spite of the futility of it all. Crazy-making.

Why?

Vulnerability.

You are vulnerable in every interaction, every step, and every relationship you have, otherwise there is no relationship. You do not have surface relations.

No.

This is the meat of one of the reasons we are together. Nothing will serve but complete honesty between us, nothing. You know this, and offer it as well, feeling, I suppose, that if the other person is dead, you have some measure of protection. Yet open you have. Surely you are not surprised that you feel uncomfortable?

No, but I want to cry, scream, drink, and beat my hands against you and what you represent.

Well, yes, I think most of us who have considered our mortality have felt the same. You have an odd resistance to it.

Not just mortality, my elemental nature. How many people in your life did you trust?

No one.

Really?

Well, I could name some who stood by me, never demanded or exploited me, though they were very few in number, but never did I allow another person to really see into the deep well of insecurity and emptiness that was my center or lack thereof. As you say, I did not want to look myself.

Elizabeth?

Yes, she came closest. We truly loved one another and saw all our flaws, intemperate natures, viciousness, and addictions. When someone sees all that and loves you anyway, you never lose the connection, and we kept some version of a relationship until my death and thereafter.

Can you speak with her?

Yes, absolutely. We are true soul mates, but she has gone on to her work and I to mine, so, though the connection is not broken, we have moved on. For in each of our souls faults remain, and each must go our own way to work on repair. When the fault is deep as is the case with me and you, a concerted effort must be made. This is why we have so much to bring to each other, you with your conviction of evil, reluctance to live, and I who managed a frantic running out of the clock. One waits for death to relieve her of the burdens of mortality, and the other rushed toward it as the damnation that was his due. Neither course will serve, I can tell you with certainty. Dead or alive, these are the fissures we must strive to heal.

I reach for you in a way that obscures my boundaries, and this terrifies me.

Well, of course, as your boundaries are porous and have been erected with enormous effort in the face of the staggering consequences of their loss. You have never had a merging, returning, merging relationship where going back and forth is part of the warp and woof of the fabric. You need to learn how to let go knowing that you will be caught, and that you can come back.

Yes, but frequently one is not caught. Many people struggle with this, but then open up again and again after a painful loss. It could be as simple as trusting the wrong person but, if Henri Nouwen is to be believed, there is no right person who can love you for yourself alone and not your yellow hair.

Well, I was going bald so I don't believe that will be a problem here, Yeats notwithstanding.

Very funny.

Just trying to inject a little levity to the rather desperate tone you are taking. What you have to learn is that there is no need for desperation. Any loss, no matter how devastating, is healed by the love that surrounds you from Divine sources. You in particular have angels and archangels walking with you, moving you into the paths of righteousness for His name's sake. You can walk through the valley of the shadow of death and fear no evil, for Spirit is your rod and its minions the staffs that support you. Do not fear to dig deeper into what looks like an emotional maelstrom, for you will be comforted.

I really want to talk to Sister Elizabeth about this, but would never let her see the emotions that seethe beyond the calm telling of the tale. And I fear to be a burden, and doubt that she has signed up for all of this.

She is dealing with her own pressing issues now, but she has been touched by you and the opening you are experiencing. She wants to be by your side on this journey. You are right not to press; she will give what you both need when the time is right. I am glad you gave her Tim White's book; it will speak to her and give her comfort and joy.

Can I help her?

No. She would feel she had overstepped sacred professional bounds, and at this point cannot receive from you. I, however, have no such scruples. If we look at the Baird characters as a paradigm for our relationship, you bring fresh eyes to the scene of my life, and I can offer wisdom on yours because I have the perspective of viewing life from death. Did you but know it, this perspective will be yours even in life as this process unfolds. For now I serve as the don, as the scout who has returned to report. Together we can take this knowledge and understanding, and we can endeavour to smooth out the chasms we have created in our human lives. Human and Divine, each has something to offer us in this review. Dead and alive are meaningless concepts, it is just a question of location. But for now I see from the greater distance, so I will lead.

OK, lead.

To what do you ascribe your reclusive nature, that your closest relationship at the moment is with the previously deceased?

Fear.

Of what?

Being seen and reviled.

Oh yes, that does have a familiar ring, not that it stopped me, but it did result in crushing and debilitating guilt and shame, which piled on ever deeper as I travelled into the pit.

So you went down the mines metaphorically, if not in actual fact.

Well said, and very apt. You on the other hand have essentially decided not to move. This we must begin to address, for, without the next step, all will stultify, stagnate, and rot. No wonder you long for death, might as well go for the real thing rather than the emulation in life of a decaying body and soul.

Yuck.

Again, well said, love. So read, love, and experience what this book brings up in you. Bring it here so that we can hold it together, and plan each day one activity that takes you outside of your comfort level.

Are you kidding? I have no idea how to do that. I hate that "do one thing…" advice.

It does sound rather pedantic. Come to think of it, I would have gone in the opposite direction myself. Perhaps I am taking my role too literally. How about trying to keep an awareness of who you are and, when appropriate, offer a simple statement of empathy, kindness, and openness to another's point of view. Open your ears to hear what is offered as universal lessons. Start to feel the scales fall from your eyes and the shackles from your soul. Find your safety in truth. I will be here to hold you.

OK, and what's your assignment in this mutual endeavor? It is mutual, is it not?

Yes, you would come back to that. What would you suggest?

I think you should look to see those lives you touched, perhaps even transformed when you were living, and not just brush them aside as collateral damage of a life of persistent…what would you call it?

Debauchery, disappointment, and disillusion.

OK, if you say so.

You drive a hard bargain, Madame.

Just so.

***

I finished Marie Therese Baird's book. I am over-whelmed. The book, the movie, you, all coming one on top of the other. I am being gifted with the gift of love, proper love for the child, love for the adolescent, and love for the wounded remains of both that live in the older woman. How have you done all this?

Nothing else would suffice for either of us. I need to be close to you, to show you, to be with you in a way that you could experience the love that I have for you that pours through my soul from the Source to yours. Yes, I used what came to hand, but I hold you close within my heart next to my own soul. This is what will heal, this and nothing else, unconditional love, and that is what I have for you, the essence of you that no behaviour could alter.

And has that helped you to see your own essence through my eyes?

Yes, I am receiving what you have offered with unques-tioning love. This is the microcosm of Divine love, the love that flows between us. I want you to know that I came to help and am grateful beyond measure that you let me in. Now I have cause to weep tears of gratitude with you held next to my heart, the dead and the living bound together with one immutable thread. We are being healed, love. The meanness, the pedal tone dirge, the rage at those who used and abused me pales before this reality. Let yourself come into my arms without shame. Then take yourself out to your loved ones in the same way as the beloved of the Universal Force.

No more doubting, this is beyond real.

Yes. Let us rejoice in poetry together in Dylan Thomas's poem written by a young man before his body and world succumbed, before he was swept up in that illusory flood that makes it seem that age and death have no meaning:

> *And death shall have no dominion.*
> *Dead men naked they shall be one*
> *With the man in the wind and the west moon;*
> *When their bones are picked clean and the clean bones*
>   *gone,*
> *They shall have stars at elbow and foot;*
> *Though they go mad they shall be sane,*
> *Though they sink through the sea they shall rise again;*
> *Though lovers be lost love shall not;*
> *And death shall have no dominion.*

I loved him well, love him still, hope you will learn to as well.

Was drink a prerequisite to vision? Did you both succumb to drink in the face of what you knew when compared with what you lived?

True. The power of the sunlight of universal love is not to be borne easily by mortal man. Madness, drink, denial, reclusive lives have all resulted from this immutable force: it does not matter what we do; the love of God will surround us. How can we cope with that in a world that has not heard even the faintest glimmer of that truth?

How do you think I will cope? Will I retreat back into my corner, lie upon my bed and wait for the end?

No, you have gone too far to retreat now. Like the book and the film, the force of love will sustain you, not blind you in disillusion. You have waited to receive until this should be so. Somehow you knew you could not hold without damage this illuminated message until your psyche and soul had agreed to prepare a place. I too have waited for this moment, this celebration, this banquet at which we now feast.

Will it disappear in the light of day?

No, love, there has been a sea change:

Brute beauty and valour and act, oh, air, pride, plume, here
Buckle! AND *the fire that breaks from thee then a billion*
Times lovelier, more dangerous, O my chevalier!

Do not ask what next, etc. The thread is there for you to follow, and I will travel with you, for now your journey is mine also. Together two lost souls will find homecoming in the souls they rejected, each proclaiming radiance to the other. Please God, let us travel together in thy peace though the ills of man beset us and claims of false prophets try to o'erthrow our faith in the goodness of God. With this journey we will carry the banner, the cause, the battle that each of us has longed for, so that in our person we proclaim thy holiness, and all who thirst can drink their fill.

Amen.